Leading the Flow

A Crash Course in Officiating Ceremonies with Confidence

Courtney Baldwin

For The Officiants of The Future

Dear Readers,

Thank you from the depths of my heart for choosing Part 1 "Leading the Flow: A Crash Course in Officiating Ceremonies with Confidence." I am truly honored to be a part of your officiating journey, and I hope this book will provide you with the knowledge and confidence to lead beautiful ceremonies that touch hearts.

I understand that stepping into the role of an officiant can be both exciting and challenging. For those of you who may need additional assistance or wish to dive deeper into this wondrous world, I offer mentorship programs designed to support you every step of the way.

I am committed to nurturing a thriving community of officiants, and that's why I've made it easy to connect with me. You can find, follow, and get in touch with me on YouTube under "Authentically Courtney," where I share valuable tips and insights. Also, connect with me on Instagram and Facebook pages by searching "Abundant Notary Services," where I'll be thrilled to engage with you and create lasting connections.

Once again, thank you for choosing "Leading the Flow." Your dedication to this craft inspires me, and I look forward to witnessing your officiating journey bloom into something truly remarkable.

With love and gratitude,

Courtney Baldwin

TABLE OF CONTENTS

SO YOU WANT TO MARRY PEOPLE? ?

So the most commonly asked question is if you are a notary, do you need to be ordained to perform ceremonies? The short answer is no, BUT remember this additional step is taken for you and not your future couples.

There are only 3 states that allow notaries to marry couples, (Florida, South Carolina and Maine) vs being ordained where you can perform a ceremony in any state.

Think about expansion, you may move and you don't want to feel limited by the sanctions of your stamp. Being ordained means you can marry couples in any state; however, Nevada and New York may require the minister to become licensed in their state. The states as well as their fees have been listed in the back of the book for referencing.

While others simply require that you be a license minister. You become ordained through companies like Universal Life Church or American Marriage Ministries. Feel free to look up the requires in your state to ensure these companies are recognized as it can vary by state.

For instance, North Carolina does not recognize ministers ordained or authorized by the universal life church to perform weddings. Law requires ministers to be ordained or authorized by a church, synagogue, mosque temple or other religious bodies in order to legally perform weddings. It is advisable to contact the local county clerks for the wedding requirements.

"What is your why?"

Standing in front of couples along with their friends and family may seem a bit intimidating to some. For introverts, it's definitely going to take a bit of courage and some practice.

So knowing your reasons behind your desire to perform ceremonies will give you momentum to push through when times are slow.

By taking these next steps to pursue wedding services you must understand the importance of your role in the lives of each couple.

Realize you are agreeing to be apart of a day that will forever be remembered by the couple long after you have moved on. How would you like to be remembered?

Are you ready for this?

Performing a ceremony isn't hard! Seriously it's all in your mind, the couples will always be more nervous than you! It's your job to be calm and in control of the day moment by moment.

When a couple books your services it can be for a number of reasons, sometimes it's last minute and you were the first one on Google! But whatever the reason may be, your goal is to leave an unforgettable impression.

Here we will focus on how you show up for yourself and thus making your presence and business unforgettable.

Don't worry about the how, that's why you purchased this e-book to learn more about the role you seek to play.

Your Ideal Couple, Let's Talk About It!

Let's talk your first ceremony, what are the initial steps to take towards getting your first couple?

I recommend starting small with eloping couples, this will allow you to perfect your skills and get over the nervousness that may come with your first time reading your script. These intimate gatherings offer an opportunity to practice delivering ceremonies, critiquing your speaking style, and building confidence in your role as a celebrant.

Your ideal starter ceremony should be small, maybe 5 to 10 people at maximum.. especially if you are an introvert. This enables you to be at ease and find comfort in speaking in front of strangers. Officiants can begin by reaching out to friends, family, or acquaintances who are planning a small-scale wedding.

Some officiants have offered their services free of charge to gain experience, reviews and build their portfolio. Join local wedding groups, Facebook groups can be helpful for both pointers and advertisement.

By starting with small ceremonies and actively seeking opportunities, you can grow your experience and confidence, setting the foundation for a successful and fulfilling career as a wedding celebrant.

Take moment to breathe, take a deep breath. Breathing properly provides you with a greater sense of mental clarity. It helps you sleep better, reduce stress and it even improves your body's immune response. Don't believe me? Google it!

Breathing is most important for you and your future couples, you have no idea what runs through their minds as they stand before you at the altar. You breathe and it helps to have them take a few deep breaths with you. Trust me, they appreciate the moment of calm.

Your breathing is also about you having control over the flow of the moments at the altar. Whether the couple is standing before you for a few moments or 30 minutes, you control the flow.

You can control the flow by being aware of the punctuations and pauses within your script. Don't worry, we'll discuss this later in the sections to follow.

Things to Know

Marriage License

Alright, so a quick chat about paperwork. The license has to be requested by the couple prior to the ceremony being held. There is a 3 day hold from the date the form is received. This means the couple cannot be married until 3 days after completing the marriage application. Small caveat, there is NO wait time for out of state couples. Licenses are valid statewide, but must be returned to the county of which the application was requested.

Licenses must be mailed or returned within 10 days of the ceremony being completed. IF the couple is out of state (to Florida), there is **NO** hold and the couple can obtain the license and marry on the same day should they wish. Check your state to determine best practices.

Keep in mind it is only valid for 60 days. Always, always, **always** check the date and confirm the names against the photo IDs. Noncitizens can use their alien registration number to verify identity as well as apply for license.

**Find an example of how to complete the license in the bonus section at the end of the book!

Flow of Ceremony

The Processional - Family & Wedding party come down the aisle
- Bride's mother, groom, best man, wedding party, flower girl, ring bearer, then bride and escort.

Welcome and Introduction - Thank guests for coming

Readings - if applicable, officiant introduces each reading & reader

Vows - Address couple, speak on importance of marriage & vow exchange

Ring Exchange - Say a few words about ring symbolism

The First Kiss - the couples exchange first affection as married couple

Final Blessings/Closing Remarks - Give encouraging words and bless union

The Recessional - pronounce couple as married & introduce couple

Types of Ceremonies

Elopements
Civil Weddings
Micro-Weddings
Traditional Weddings
Non-religious Weddings
Spiritual Weddings
Ambush/Surprise
Weddings

Civil Weddings – Non-religious ceremonies, officiated by government authorities. Focuses more on the legal aspects of marriage, normally includes simple vows and license signing.

Cultural Weddings – Reflection of the rich heritage and values shared, a celebration of identity, community and family. May include cultural music, rituals, prayers, traditional attire and more.

Micro-Weddings –Intimate or small ceremonies with no more than 50 people. Offers couples the option of a more relaxed and meaningful day.

Non-Traditional Weddings – Personalized to couples' values and preferences, includes unique themes, vows and rituals that have special meaning to the couple.

Interfaith Weddings – Blends elements of two or more religions to include diverse backgrounds as unique the couple. The ceremony is designed to bring honor to and celebrate unity within diversity.

Religious Weddings – Follow the custom and religion specific rituals, ie Jewish, Muslim, Catholic, Hindu, Buddhist, Christian, etc etc. May involve prayers, sacred readings, blessings, and other religion specific rituals.

Spiritual Weddings – Focuses on celebrating couples 'connection on a more soulful level. May include mediation, mindfulness, affirmations, blessings or anything that resonates with couple's beliefs.

Vow Renewals – Celebration of couple's ongoing commitment to one another

Attire

What you wear is a major part of the couple's special day, not just because of the pictures! Normally officiants and minister wear black as to blend in BUT ask your couples what they would like. I also recommend dressing for the venue, some weddings can be upscale and elegant, and you'll want to ask the couples about the location.

Some couples may request that you dress in their wedding colors as not to stick out among photos. Ladies this means nothing too tight or anything that may take attention away from the brides! Also wear if you choose heels, wear a pair that is comfortable just in case there is a bit more walking.

Gentleman, if a tie and jacket are required, please be mindful as well, a good belt and matches shoes will do! Otherwise, a nice crisp shirt and slacks will compliment any day

Equipment

In most cases it is up to the wedding officiant may chose not to use a microphone but depending on the venue or location it is recommended. For instance, a ceremony in the park or on the beach the acoustics may not be the best and your voice will be interrupted by the surrounding elements. When in doubt, be prepared! There are different types of microphones to fit any occasion. But the most important thing is to ensure that your voice is clear and audible during the ceremony.

I have listed a few of the popular microphones to better assist you with understanding the types and their usages. But do your research on which one would best suit your officiating style.

Lavalier - Affectionately known as the "lapel" is a small microphone that is clipped on clothing, normally the collar. Keeps your hands free while you hold your script or the couples' rings, (yes sometimes you will hold things).

Handheld - As the title states, the officiant will hold this microphone and pass it around to the couple if needed during vows. Some may offer a comfortable grip, or you may opt for the microphone necklace to keep your hands free.

Headset - This particular microphone is positioned on your head and the microphone is maneuvered as close to your mouth as possible. This microphone will keep your hands free while offering consistent sound throughout your ceremonies.

Bodypack Transmitter - This setup involves the officiant wearing a bodypack transmitter and a clip-on microphone that is attached to your clothing. Small note, placing the bodypack underneath clothing helps with cleaner pictures for your couple(s).

Shotgun Microphone - This type focuses primarily on the officiants voices and minimizes background noises. You will often find these on a stand or attached to a camera for best sound.

Wireless Microphone- The wireless option allows you to move freely without the confinement of cables. Wireless systems consist of a transmitter (attached to the microphone) and a receiver (connected to the sound system).

Combo systems - Some wireless systems offer both a handheld microphone and a bodypack transmitter with the option to connect different microphone types. This means you can switch between both if needed.

Booking your first couple

Where to market yourself

Woo, here comes the fun part! Figuring out where to show up is as simple as listing your services on your Google Business Page.

If you have the funds to pay for platforms like Thumbtack, WeddingWire, Brides.com, The Knot or Wedding Pro, either can work but they can be quite pricey and can eat away at your profit.

Try posting on social media first, putting ads in your local newspaper, word of mouth works as well and the best part... All of them are free. You may also consider visiting venues,
messaging vendors and leaving cards at bridal shops.

Let's not forget wedding directories, local wedding expos (cheaper than major expos), blogging, Google My Business, wedding magazines, YouTube, collaborations with other wedding vendors, offering free workshops or seminars related to the wedding industry.

Remember, consistency and a strong online presence are keys to successful marketing. Ensure that your approach is tailored to your target client and be patient with yourself building a reputation is not a quick process.

Vendor Networking

The importance of networking with other weddings vendors cannot be overstated. Collaborations and connections are major keys to create a memorable experience for your couples. These relationships can also be vital when attempting to book your first wedding!

Working with vendors can enhance the wedding experience for your couples and also create future referrals for your business! Introduce yourself to any vendors you have not met prior to performing the ceremony or speak with them afterwards. Don't forget to pass out your cards!

Couples like officiants who are well connected, it speaks volumes about being an experienced and reputable professional. This allows you to build trust, increase reach and visibility, gain opportunities and insights from other vendors, as well as build a close-knit community for your business.

Find a list of selected vendors in the bonus pages

Interacting with Your Couple

Interacting with couples prior to booking a wedding is crucial for building trust and establishing a strong foundation for a successful working relationship.

Interacting with couples allows you to establish a personal connection with them. Through conversations, you can understand the couple's vision, preferences, and expectations for their wedding ceremony. Clear communication helps alleviate doubts and uncertainties. You can address any concerns or questions the couple might have about your role, the ceremony, or your expertise.

Any conversations you have with your couple(s) will provide an opportunity to showcase your expertise and offer insights into creating a meaningful and memorable ceremony. Couples often look to wedding officiants for guidance and this is where you can offer suggestions, share ideas, and help them make informed decisions. This rapport not only builds trust but helps minimize the chances of miscommunication or misunderstandings that could lead to issues on the wedding day.

Interviewing your couple

Consider your first consultation call an interview, you're getting to know your couple and their desires for their wedding day. Before you can create your script, you must learn your couples' love story and the vision they have for their special day.

However, you accomplish this is up to you I recommend creating a list of questions or finding a questionnaire that will provide the answers you will need to prepare.

Pricing

Some may feel that learning how to price their services is the most important part of this business but they'd be wrong! Having services worth booking is the first and most important chunk of your business. Remember, many couples are already nervous about other aspects of their ceremony but your job is to ensure your services are the smoothest and easiest to book.

Remember you lack experience and want to charge according to the service you will provide. The higher you charge, the more services you will be expected to offer. It's recommended that you start your services at the lower end, $100- $300, not including travel.

However, determining your price margin you will want to review others in your industry because you know.. Research.

The average cost of an officiant is anywhere between $500 to $800 and this is before add-ons or premarital counseling. However, there are expectations that go along with charging $500 a ceremony.

The e-book is going to give a foundation to start with so that your services can measure up!

Your prices are all about the services you can provide within your packaging. Before thinking about the money, determine what you bring to the table and what you would like to offer your couples. How much time will you be investing in perfecting your skills and talents to add to their services?

Have more to offer than just your script, couples love options, this is how you can set yourself apart from your competition. Options can include: sand ceremonies, unity candle ceremonies, ring warming, or hand blessings.

Believe it or not, your success is directly affected by the amount of time you speed investing in growing yourself and your skills. How can you personalize each ceremony by offering the talents you already possess? Your services dictate your price margin, not the market you're in.

We all have that special something that sets us apart from everyone else, once you establish your anchor in this industry your business will thrive!

Closing the Deal

This is where you help the clients to see why they need your services. Will you offer a custom script? Do you specialize in small or traditional weddings? Here is where you stand out and shine, explain as well as provide examples of what you can bring to make their wedding special. Don't know where to start, no worries... There's help in the bonus pages!

Alright, you've booked them, now what?

TAKE A DEEP BREATH

Yes, breathe honey this is where the ball keeps rolling. So now, let's talk scripts! There are plenty of scripts out on the internet to get you started but know that some couples are looking for a bit more than samples from the web.

Your script should represent your couples, this means that it should feel like them, like their love story and you can create it! How? Use a questionnaire to familiarize yourself with the couple and their story. Ask them how they would like their ceremony to feel, like what takeaways do they want to remember from the day. Everyone has a dream and a story; your job is to put it to paper in a way that's all your own!

Not a writer? That's okay, there are script generators out there as well as professional writers who can help with that! Need more guidance, contact me I can help with that.

To Vow or Not to Vow

LEGAL REQUIREMENTS

You may come across couples who only want someone to sign their license without a ceremony or vows exchanges. While you want to fulfill the requests of your couples, you must also ensure that the marriage is legal in the eye of the law.

During the ceremony, the officiant will ask the couple a legal question that confirms their intent to marry. This question typically goes along the lines of, "Do you [partner's name], take [other partner's name], to be your lawfully wedded spouse?" The partners respond with "I do" or "I will."

No matter how short the vow exchange may be, it is your sole responsibility to ensure both parties have the intent to marry. This legal intent is important because it signifies their willingness to undertake certain responsibilities and rights that come with being married. Vow or no vows, intent is one of the most important parts of your role.

Scripts & Readings

PUTTING FOREVER ON PAPER

A well-worded script is vital for wedding officiants as it forms the foundation of a meaningful and memorable wedding ceremony. Here's why:

1. **Structure and Flow**: A script provides a structured outline for the ceremony, guiding the officiant and ensuring a smooth flow from one segment to another.
2. **Meaningful Content**: A script allows the officiant to include meaningful and personalized content that reflects the couple's values, beliefs, and love story.
3. **Consistency**: A script helps maintain consistency throughout the ceremony, ensuring that key elements, rituals, and sentiments are included.
4. **Professionalism**: A well-prepared script demonstrates professionalism and reassures the couple that the officiant is knowledgeable and well-prepared.
5. **Confidence**: Having a script to follow boosts the officiant's confidence, reducing the likelihood of stumbling over words or forgetting important elements.
6. **Guidance**: A script offers guidance on transitions, cues, and timing, helping the officiant lead the ceremony seamlessly.
7. **Legal Requirements**: A script can include legal vows or statements required for the marriage to be legally binding.

Script Execution

DELIVERING IN EXCELLENCE

Your goal as an officiant is to create a heartfelt and memorable experience for the couple and their guests. But ultimately however you choose to deliver is totally up to you!

Some officiants have chosen to fully memorize the script which allows for a more natural delivery. You could memorize key points, opening words, vows or closing remarks and this would still result in authenticity and accuracy. Should you so choose, summarization is also an option to highlight the most important factors. But if you divvy away from the script a couple has agreed you want to be mindful of their reaction(s).

Cue cards can be a Godsend if your memory isn't the best, there are also tablets to enable to reference your script when needed. If you're old school and would prefer to hold your script, bring a backup just in case it rains! Trust me, you will kick yourself if you have to emprise because your script gets wet!

The choice between memorization, summarization, or referencing tools depends on your comfort level, experience, and the desired tone of the ceremony. Delivering a memorable ceremony is always the goal, determine which option will best help you achieve this goal and start there! Remember, as you gain experience, you will evolve.

Contracts

Another important document is a contract, while one is recommended, they are not required. They provide a clear and legally binding framework that outlines the terms, expectations, and responsibilities of both the officiant and the couple getting married.

A well-drafted contract specifies all the details related to the wedding ceremony, including the date, time, location, and any special requests or requirements. The contract should also clearly define the fee structure, payment schedule, and any additional charges. This clarity helps prevent conflicts regarding the services provided and the associated costs.

This contract should address these scenarios, outlining the terms for cancellations, rescheduling, and any applicable refunds or fees. Contracts also explain the following: deposits and payments, liabilities and responsibilities, contingencies, dispute resolution and ownership of intellectual property (personalized vows, ceremony, script, and other content).

Find a sample contract in the bonus pages

Let's Talk Money!

In a world of technology, you must know how to collect payments in all forms. Invoices can be created and sent using many different platforms. There are also various methods to accepting payment such as: Stripe, Venmo, Zelle, Square, Apple Pay and many others.

When requesting payment, wedding officiants should provide clear and concise instructions, including the payment amount, due date, preferred payment method, and any necessary account or contact information. They can also consider sending a confirmation receipt once the payment has been received to ensure transparency and accountability.

Invoices & Payments

Imagine showing up to a ceremony, completing your services and not receiving payment for any of it! Believe it or not, many officiants have experienced couples not completing their final payment long after the ceremony has been completed. This is where your contract would come in handy because it breaks down the specifics of the ceremony, including the payment deadline.

You should never perform services without receiving full payment for the ceremony. Rule of thumb, one month prior to the ceremony date couples should have the final draft of their ceremony script and within one week before to the ceremony date all payments should be made. No matter how small the wedding, your time matters and you should be compensated.

Here are some payment options and ways to request payment:

1. Cash or Check
2. Bank Transfer
3. PayPal or Other Payment Platforms
4. Venmo or Mobile Payment Apps:(Venmo, Cash App, or Apple Pay)
5. Credit Card Payment
6. Online Invoicing
7. Contract and Deposit
8. Payment Requests via Email
9. Payment Request Forms on Website
10. Square or Card Readers

Ceremonies for Inmates

Yes, it's a thing and it may not be for everyone but, here's how to do it right!

Ensure you familiarize yourself with the following processes as well as determine your pricing for safety (any lock down/safety fees should be refundable if no lock down occurs during ceremony). I charge a $50 fee and refund it as soon as I have made it back to my car safely. This is disclosed to my couple(s) prior to final payment.

Know The Rules
Understand the rules and limitations, for instance there are limits on guests, ceremony time frame, and items allowed beyond the metal detectors.

It's essential to be sensitive to the couple's desires but also operate within the constraints of the facility. When at all possible, opt for a simple and meaningful ceremony keeping any restraints in mind.

It is recommended, if at all possible to conduct a rehearsal prior to the day of to ease nerves and ensure the ceremony day runs smoothly.

Obtaining Permission

Before couples can begin planning their ceremony, permission must be granted by the proper authorities. Each institution has their own set guidelines and requirements. You might need to undergo a background check and provide documentation, such as your identification, credentials, and any necessary licenses.

Call the institution to gain a better understanding of their process. Provide information about the event, your role as the officiant, and any relevant credentials. Normally, the Chaplin can be a great source of information and guidance.

Dress Code

The facility may restrict certain attire or accessories, be mindful of this and speak with the proper authorities to ensure you dress appropriately. Ladies, no cleavage but most importantly forget the wire bra and thank me later! Gents, be prepared to empty your pockets and take off your belts, bracelets and/or watches.

Follow all the security protocols to make the process smooth and hassle free.

Marriage License

Processing the marriage license is the same as previously mentioned. If the couple has witnesses, (if your state requires it) have them sign after you have performed the ceremony. Thereafter the license needs to be returned to the courts for processing.

Photography and Recording

Even though this is a special day, normally phones and recording items are not permitted in correctional facilities. Be sure to ask the lead authority on the policies are surrounding this subject.

Remember, it is important to ensure all post-ceremony arrangements are approved by the facilitators or carried out off the premises.

Approach this task with empathy, professionalism and be committed to creating a meaningful and respectful ceremony.

Tips

Respectful Language: Use respectful and inclusive language throughout the ceremony.

Sensitivity: Keep in mind the emotional stress the participants might be under due to their circumstances. Be empathetic and understanding.

Time Limit: Corrections facilities often have strict time limits for events. Ensure your ceremony fits within the allocated time.

Maintain Control: Maintain control over the proceedings. Avoid any behavior or content that could disrupt the facility's security or cause any distress to inmates, staff, or other participants.

Exit the Facility: Once the ceremony is concluded, follow the facility's exit procedures, which might involve another security check.

Communication: Maintain open communication with the facility staff to ensure everyone is on the same page regarding rules, expectations, and procedures.

Flexibility: Be flexible and adaptable, as the facility's rules and requirements may change on short notice.

Arrive Early: Arrive well in advance to allow time for security procedures and any last-minute adjustments.

Stay Professional: Maintain a professional demeanor throughout the process. This helps build rapport with both facility staff and participants.

Remember, it is important to ensure all post-ceremony arrangements are approved by the facilitators or carried out off the premises. Approach this task with empathy, professionalism and be committed to creating a meaningful and respectful ceremony.

An inclusive wedding officiant understands the importance of incorporating love in all its forms. Love is a universal language; every couple's love story is unique and a wedding is a perfect example of this.

A compassionate officiant will help not only make a memorable ceremony for the couple but also create a more accepting world.

Here's a list why being inclusive is important:

1. Respecting Diversity
2. Fosters Inclusivity
3. Empowers Couples
4. Relfects the Changing of Times
5. Supports Marriage Equality

Ways to Include all types of love:

1. Gender-Neutral Language
2. Personalized Ceremonies
3. Embrace Cultural Traditions
4. Openness to Non-Religious Ceremonies
5. Acknowledgment of LGBTQ+ Love
6. Inclusive Readings and Vows
7. Pronoun Check-In
8. Be Respectful and Non-Judgmental

As a wedding officiant, it is not only important to secure the couple and their wedding date but also solidify their confidence in your abilities to respect their way of life.

This means using language in the ceremony script and communication materials to ensure the couple is well represented. Also, consider offering personalized ceremonies, this will allow them to include any cultural or religions tradition that may be meaningful to them.

Learn about various types of practices and customs so that upon request you can include them in your ceremonies. Express your support for the LGBTQIA+ couples, if you consider yourself an ally, make it apparent on your website and marketing materials.

Offering diverse readings, poems and quotes that celebrate different types of love will be a winner for any couple. Listen to your couples' story, doing so will help you understand their unique preferences and backgrounds. This is how we create a ceremony that truly reflects who they are.

Building a network of inclusive wedding vendors is helpful because it may lead to referrals and collaborations on diverse weddings. Being an inclusive wedding officiant is demonstrated by your level of commitment to celebrating all types of love and creating a welcoming environment for diverse couples. What type of wedding officiant do you want to be?

Preparing for the Ceremony

As you approach the couple's special day there are quite a few boxes you will need to check in order to be properly prepared. Think about what type of impression you would like to leave on not just the couple but also their friends and family. You may want to leave your business cards or bring the couple a thoughtful gift.

Things to Do

The days leading up to the ceremony are the most crucial for a wedding officiant. Regular communication is necessary to answer questions, provide couple with guidance, and make any last minute adjustments to the script.

Any changes made to the script need to be finalized prior to the ceremony, if this can be arranged. Please note, couples may have last minute changes on the day of the wedding as well. Rule of thumb, always bring a pen just in case you need to make any last minute changes.

More things to add to your checklist:
- Confirm the time and location
- Confirm the person you will be checking in with
- Check the pronunciation of names (first and last names)
- Remind the couple to bring their marriage license and photo identification
- Test your microphone
- Offer support and reassurance to the couple
- Review your script, practice speaking confidently, and learn a good pace
- Stay organized, keep any notes or scripts together
- Get to know the venue, be familiar with the location

Rehearsals

Each couple you book may not require you to attend their rehearsals or may choose to skip this option all together! But just in case they do and you are invited, here are a few tips!

This invite ensures you will meet the wedding party, most of the family and friends, prior to the day of the ceremony. Trust me, it's a major plus! By attending you will have a chance to iron out the small details as well as collect your nerves in a calm setting. So kick back, (not to much though you're still the professional), share in the laughs, and enjoy the experience.

While couples may not require your attendance, a wedding planner may request it but it is not a requirement. It will make it easy to understand the line up and flow of the bridal party as they begin walking down the aisle. Keep in mind that you will, (normally) be the first to arrive at the altar.

This is also a go place to show the guests and bridal party your professionalism and personality while mingling. You may be invited to the dinner afterwards, you determine where you will spend your time. No pressure.

**Remember, this is your personal time and you may or may not choose to charge extra for your attendance. This matter is up to you, my rate is $75 for rehearsals.

Receptions

We can't touch on rehearsals without discussing the reception as well! When an officiant attends the reception it's far more than simply to enjoy the festivities. It's an opportunity to foster connections, expand your network, and demonstrate your commitment to creating meaningful and memorable experiences for couples. By being present and engaged, you can grow your business through word-of-mouth, collaborations, and a strong online presence, ultimately establishing yourself as a trusted and sought-after wedding officiant.

Keepsakes

Consider whether or not you would like to offer commemorative certificates for couples to sign as a memento of their special day. Ceremonial marriage certificates are the normal keepsakes to give couples, it gives them something to sign after the "I Dos" have concluded.

Some may also opt to give their couples vow books, ornaments (to celebrate their first Christmas), key chains. custom air freshener with the couple's engagement photo or a personalize memory box. The idea is to set yourself apart from other officiants; it gives your couple something to brag about when discussing or recommending your services.

Day of Ceremony

Let's discuss preparation! Showing up an hour in advance is the recommended time frame but an hour and a half would allow for weather or traffic issues. Equally consider how do you plan on preparing for the day. Will you have a playlist that gets you pumped while singing your heart out to warm up those vocals? Will you listen to motivational speeches or affirmations to help get you in the right mindset? Remember, you are in charge of your day and the ceremony, how would you like to be prepared for it?

Prep the night before, have the script ready, place all the things you'll need for ceremony together, determine your attire, accessories (if applicable), check your car tires, and engine... Oh, and last but not least fill up your gas tank! These are just a few things that can cause you to be late or stall the flow of your day. Be careful, not all couples are forgiving of mistakes or waiting for you.

What To Do When You Have Arrived

01 In my questionnaires, I ask couples who I should check in with upon arrival and they usually name a person (if it's not an elopement) for me to speak with. Find this person and introduce yourself.

02 No one will know you are an officiant until you tell them, some choose to where a name tag but definitely mingle with the guests! Also, introduce yourself to other vendors, shake hands, leave your cards on table and chairs... Don't let them forget your name or face!

03 Once you have finished mingling, find a quiet place or space to look over your script a few times. Steps 1-2 should take you about 10-30 minutes depending on the size of the wedding, (this is why we arrive early). Step 3 helps you read less and connect more with the guests more. Besides, how will you know where the photographer is if your head is down? Don't forget to look up and smile, you got this!

04 Now it's show time! While standing at the altar with the groom, take a deep breath. Look around and smile at the guests, make small talk with the groom. Once the bride arrives, have them both take a few breathes with you. Remember you control the flow of the ceremony, and the script is already written.

Finishing Strong

Alright, so you've performed the ceremony and the couple has gone off for pictures... What's next? Commemorative certificates should also be signed after the ceremony concludes and sometimes during the photoshoot! You'll lose them to the magic of the day after that!

Decide whether you would like to stay for cocktail hour and other festivities. Ultimately, it's up to you whether you stay or go but couples will offer you dinner, drinks and more.

Processing the Marriage License

The Certificate of Marriage does not require witnesses to sign but if your couple chooses, make sure it happens before the pictures... Once it has been signed by your couple, witnesses and you, it's ready to be sent for processing.

As Officiants and Ministers, it is our job to return the license to the where it was received. You can do this 1 of 3 ways, mail it back, hand deliver it or allow the couple to return it themselves.

Sending Confirmation of License

Depending on which option you selected, you may need to follow up with your couple and provide confirmation that the license has been processed. You can do this by checking the Clerk of Circuit Courts website and sending the couple a confirmation of the date processed.

However, if the couple takes it themselves this step can be skipped. Normally, the efficient returns the license but many couples may insist. As compromise, you can accompany the couple to the clerk's office. Also gives you a chance to pass your business cards out to the clerk behind the counter.

Don't Forget to Ask for Reviews

Knowing when to request reviews from your couples is key! The Honeymoon stage is real and in full effect once you leave the wedding. Make it a practice of sending your requests a few days after the ceremony.

This will allow the couple a chance to come off of their honeymoon high and get back to business. Try sending a text message, an email or a post card as a way to request their review.

Name Change Process

Many couples may ask you about changing their name and what process entitles. It is most helpful when you can answer their questions without sending them elsewhere. While the process is fairly simple, it can be a tedious process for some and having a guide from your officiant goes a long way in the grand scheme of things.

An important thing to note is that the marriage certificate will need to be processed and the certificate must be in hand prior to completing the "Petition for Change of Name" form. A guide for Florida couples wanting to change their name has been included in the bonus section of the book.

Marriage Certificate Request

A marriage certificate is essential to couples because it not only symbolizes an important day in their lives, but it also proves validity of a marriage. It is official evidence of their union and is required for not just the process listed above, but also in obtaining joint benefits, proving marital status for insurance and immigration purpose.

The marriage certificate can be requested before or after the ceremony has been held, this depends on the couples' preference. If the couple has opted to request the certificate after the ceremony, the options include in-person application, mail-requests, online applications, or over-the-phone ordering. The cost is typically under $15 unless ordering multiple copies or if the document is being expedited.

**Link and step by step guide included in bonus pages

The basics of being an Officiant or Minister are simple and may vary per state, but it is what you put into this industry that makes you and your ceremonies special.

Remember...

It is YOU who will find the couples, book them for a consultation, offer your services/available options and carry out their special day. YOU are responsible for creating a script that will capture your couple's love, setting the tone for the rest of their lives. No pressure...

However, embarking on this journey is so rewarding and being prepared will help you hit the ground running. All you need is a vision, the proper knowledge and a little help. Being a wedding vendor is more than reading a script, there will be so much more you will learn.

That is why you are here, with me finishing this e-book because you know you have a responsibility. Cheers to you for taking the next step to be a part of this wonderful industry. There are resources all around you, use everything for inspiration!

Thank you for purchasing my e-book and I hope these gems will allow your business to expand beyond your wildest dreams. Got for it and if you need backup, I can help with that!

XO
Courtney B.

Bonus Pages!

PUT A BIT OF YOURSELF IN YOUR SCRIPTS

BIBLE PASSAGE SAMPLES

Hebrews 13:4 - Let marriage be held in honor among all, and let the marriage bed be undefiled, for God will judge the sexually immoral and adulterous.

Proverbs 21:9 - It is better to live in a corner of the housetop than in a house shared with a quarrelsome wife.

1 Peter 3:7 - Likewise, husbands, live with your wives in an understanding way, showing honor to the woman as the weaker vessel, since they are heirs with you of the grace of life, so that your prayers may not be hindered.

1 John 4:7-8 ~ Beloved, let us love one another, for love is from God, and whoever loves has been born of God and knows God. Anyone who does not love does not know God, because **God is love**.

MAKE A LIST OF VENDORS TO RECOMMEND!

- [ ] Florists
- [ ] DJs
- [ ] Venues/Parks/Beach (know who requires a permit)

- [ ] Caterers
- [ ] Bartenders
- [ ] Servicers

Readings & Poems

PUT A BIT OF YOURSELF IN YOUR SCRIPTS

1. *"The Art of Marriage" by Wilferd Arlan Peterson*
2. *"Union" by Robert Fulghum*
3. *Excerpt from "The Prophet" by Khalil Gibran*
4. *"Love" by Roy Croft*
5. *"Blessing for a Marriage" by James Dillet Freeman*
6. *"On Your Wedding Day" by Unknown*
7. *"To Love is Not to Possess" by James Kavanaugh*
8. *Excerpt from "Gift from the Sea" by Anne Morrow Lindbergh*
9. *"The Promise" by Eileen Rafter*
10. *"The Master Speed" by Robert Frost*
11. *"Love is Not Love" by Elizabeth Barrett Browning*
12. *"The Invitation" by Oriah Mountain Dreamer*
13. *"I Carry Your Heart with Me" by E.E. Cummings*
14. *"The Good-Morrow" by John Donne*
15. *"The Bridge Across Forever" by Richard Bach*
16. *"The Light of Love" by Unknown*
17. *"Two" by Unknown*
18. *"The Irrational Season" by Madeleine L'Engle*
19. *"The Art of a Good Marriage" by Wilferd Arlan Peterson*
20. *"I Love You" by Roy Croft*

Couple Fact Sheet

Consultation Questionnaire

Couple names: _______ & _______

1. *Ceremony Fee Quoted: $ _________ (travel NOT included)*
2. *Best Contact Number: ___________*
3. *Date/time - _______ @ ________*
4. *Location/Venue - __________________*
5. *Flight time: ____hr ___ mins $_____ round trip*
6. *Indoor or outdoor? _______*
7. *Colors: _____ _________*
8. *How many people? ______ guest*
9. *Type of ceremony? Simple, traditional, contemporary, ___________*
10. *Add-ons/Special Request _____________*
11. *Mentions God? _______________*
12. *Will there be rings?_______*
13. *Who will hold the rings?________________*
14. *Do you have vows?________________*
15. *Need Help writing vows? _______________*
16. *Who should I check in with on arrival? (if applicable) ________ ___________*
17. *Anything tricking about finding the location? ____________________*
18. *Any special covid-19 precautions requested? (mask or shot etc) __________ required___________________*
19. *Mailing address: (if applicable) _____________________*
20. *Email address: _________________________*
21. *Describe your event:(feel, vibe, expectations, unplugged?)*

____

____

____

____

____

Vendors

WHO TO NETWORK WITH

1. *Wedding Planners*
2. *Photographers*
3. *Videographers*
4. *Florists*
5. *Venues*
6. *Caterers*
7. *DJs and Musicians*
8. *Bridal Shops*
9. *Cake Designs*
10. *Wedding Rental Companies*
11. *Hotels*
12. *Wedding Bands*
13. *Wedding Dance Instructors*
14. *Wedding Transportation*
15. *Hair and Makeup Artists*
16. *Wedding Cake Bakers/Creators*

States & Minister Requirements

1. *Alabama - A minister must be a minister of the Gospel authorized by the customs of the denomination to perform marriage ceremonies or be a rabbi or other spiritual leader of any other faith to legally perform weddings.*

2. *New York - Marriage ceremonies can be performed by ministers who are duly authorized by a religious organization and are genuinely in regular communion with the religious society to which they belong.*

3. *North Carolina - (As mentioned on page 4) Law requires ministers to be ordained or authorized by a church, synagogue, mosque temple or other religious bodies in order to legally perform weddings.*

4. *Ohio - Ministers must be licensed or ordained by a religious society or denomination to solemnize marriages.*

5. *Virginia - A minister must be ordained or authorized to celebrate the rites of marriage and should be affiliated with a religious denomination or society.*

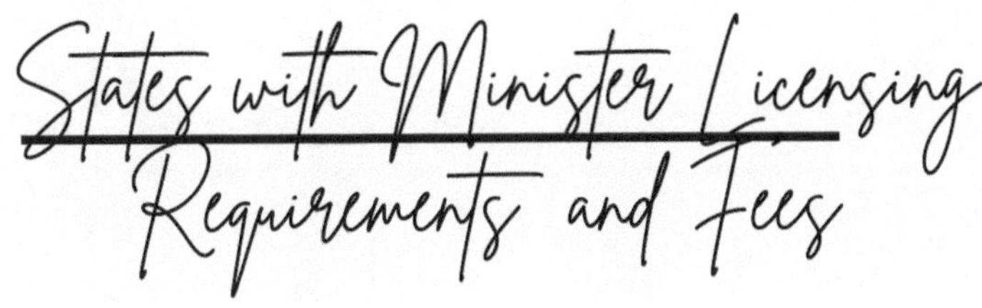

1. *Arkansas $50*

2. *Delaware $50*

3. *District of Columbia $45*

4. *Hawaii $10*

5. *Louisiana $50*

6. *Massachusetts $50*

7. *Minnesota $50*

8. *Nevada $25- $100*

9. *New Hampshire $25*

10. *New York $15*

11. *Ohio $10*

12. *Puerto Rico $25*

13. *Vermont $100*

14. *Virginia $50*

15. *West Virginia $25*

Please refer to link below for more information by state

https://getordained.org/state-marriage-laws

Marriage License Tutorial

REMEMBER:

- **Check couple's ID, ensure the names on the application match.**
- **Review effective date (3 day wait for residence)**
- **Review expiration date (60 days to marry)**

THIS IS THE MOST IMPORTANT BOX

- Line 21: What date did you officiate the date the ceremony?
- Line 22: Where did you officiate the wedding?
- Line 23a: Your signature
- Line 23b: Print your name and title, (notaries, stamp in box)
- Line 23c: Your business address
- Line 24 & 25: Witnesses (FL is optional)

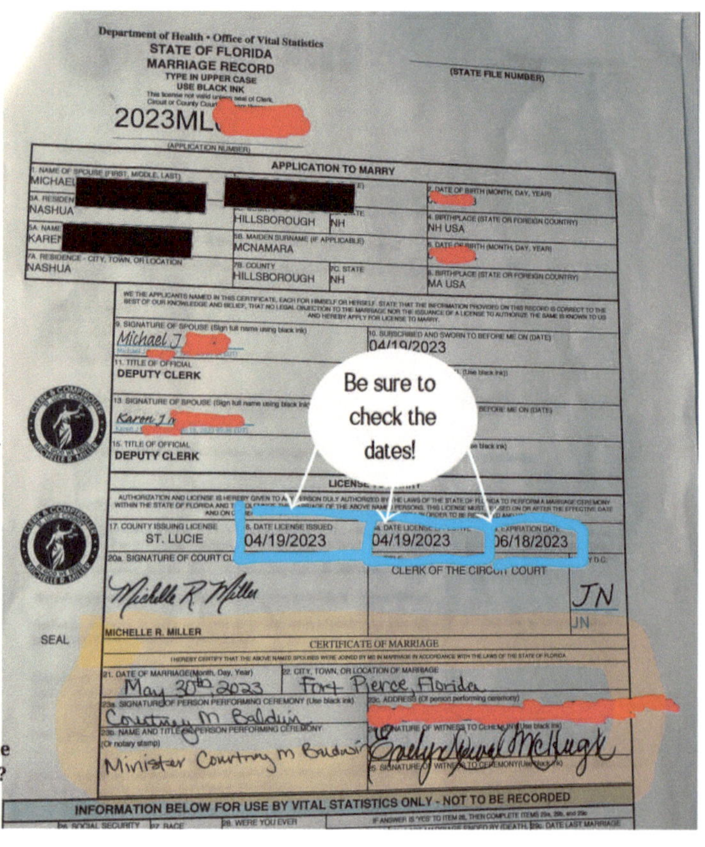

****Florida license shown above**

Need Assistance with Your First Script?

SAMPLE OF SIMPLE CEREMONY

WELCOME/INTRODUCTION

Minister: Welcome friends and family, please be seated. This is a beautiful day to gather as we celebrate and witness such love and joy shared between these two.

The marriage ceremony is the closet relationship that can exist on this earth between two people.
Today begins a new chapter, one they both deserve, and it is their desire to love each other for life and that is what we are celebrating! Friends and family, you are here to bear witness as well as be the firm foundation of the journey which led to this pivotal moment.

Today is about their devotion, love, marriage to be created by eternal promises, ones that only the two of them can keep.

OPENING PRAYER OR READING

Discuss this with your couple, some may not be religions or have elected family/friend to read poem/passage.

Share with guests the couples view on marriage and encourage significance of this commitment.
You may also include historical events which lead up to couples' arrival at the altar

Dedication Example (optional)

Marriage gives permanence and structure to a couple's love. It's a way you tell one another that no matter how much you snore or how much you spent on plants or at the mall we're still in this together!

Marriage is telling the one you love that your existence in their lives will remain the most constant among all others. It's the most powerful commitment two people can make to one another. The road that led you both here may have challenged your love, but through those challenges you have gathered strength and stand here continuing your journey in love today.

___________ and _____________I ask that you always treat yourself and each other with respect and remind yourselves often of what brought you together today. Give the highest priority to the tenderness, gentleness and kindness that your marriage deserves.

The 2 of you stand before me to affirm your love for one another, to formally acknowledge that your lives are meant to be shared as one. Know you are stronger together than you are apart, and that for all your days yet to you two will partake in all of life's joys and challenges, committed to one another.

VOW EXCHANGE

Minister:

Written Vows *(If couples does not write vows, you will need samples of your own)*
________________, please take you time and share your vows
________________, please share your vows.

To Groom
____________, do you take ____________, to live together in the union of marriage? To take him or her as your best friend and partner in life? To honor, cherish, and love him or her from this day forward, for better or for worse, for richer, for poor and sickness and in health for all your days? "I do"

Bride: I DO

To Bride
____________, do you take ____________, to live together in the union of marriage? To take him or her as your best friend and partner in life? To honor, cherish, and love him or her from this day forward, for better or for worse, for richer, for poor and sickness and in health for all your days? "I do"

Groom: I DO

RING BLESSING & EXCHANGE

Minister: The wedding rings circular shape represents the unending power of love and a source with no beginning and no end. You should wear these rings proudly and let them remind you each day of your commitment to one another.

Minister: May we have the rings please?

To the Groom
_____________, when you are ready, please repeat after me.

I _____________ give you _____________, this ring as a symbol of my love.
As I place it on your finger, I commit the whole of my heart and soul to you. I promise to cherish you for the rest of my days. I gave you all that I am and accept all that you are.

To the Bride
_____________, when you are ready, please repeat after me.

I _____________ give you _____________, this ring as a symbol of my love. As I place it on your finger, I commit the whole of my heart and soul to you. I promise to cherish you for the rest of my days. I gave you all that I am and accept all that you are.

THE KISS & FINAL WISHES

Going forward knowing that you have chosen and been chosen. You no longer walk alone through life. To make your relationship work will take love. This is the core of your
marriage and why you are here today. It will take trust, to know that in your hearts, you
truly want what is best for each other.

Be each other's teachers and know that you are surrounded by people in this very space who love you both. May you have many long years to delight in each other's love and
company. I wish you the best through every season of your lives together.

By the power vested in me, by the state of Florida, I am pleased to pronounce you are
married, sealed together today both in law and in love. _____________ and _____________, you may
seal this marriage with a kiss.

PRONOUNCE THE COUPLE & RECESSIONAL BEGINS

Full Ceremony Script Sample

SAMPLE OF CEREMONY

OPENING WORDS

Minister/Officiant:

Welcome friends and family to this day of celebration! The couple has asked that your phones be put away and or silenced at this time. They ask that you be present in this moment they have allowed you to share with them.

Friends and Family, please turn to welcome the bride... You may be seated.

It is a wonderful day to gather here in honor of the love shared between __________ and ________. Their love story began uniquely when _________ asked ________ out and he mistakenly believed it was a group outing! But that small misunderstanding creating the beautiful foundation which lead us to this very moment.

Today begins a new chapter, one they both deserve, and it is their desire to love each other for life and that is what we are celebrating! Friends and family, you are here to bear witness as well as be the firm foundation of the journey which led to this pivotal moment.

Today is about their devotion, their love, their marriage to be created by eternal promises, ones that only the two of them can keep. By standing here __________ and __________ you both are making promises to:

1. Be there for one another through whatever life may throw at you.
2. Create a good marriage by remembering the little things are the big things!
3. Be present in your union and show up each day offering your love and support to your union.
4. To forever continue the shared laughter that led you both to where your feet are planted.
5. Speak words of appreciation and demonstrate gratitude in thoughtful ways.
6. To grow together and provide a safe space for your love to endlessly blossom.
7. Walk this journey knowing that you shall age together with everlasting love for one another.

Today we share in your joyous decision to keep building an even more amazing life as a married couple.

Minister/Officiant:

I ask that you always treat yourself and each other with respect, and remind yourselves often of what brought you together today.
Give the highest priority to the tenderness, gentleness and kindness that your marriage deserves.
The 2 of you stand before me to affirm your love for one another, to formally acknowledge that your lives are meant to be shared as one.
Know you are stronger together than you are apart, and that for all your days yet to you two will partake in all of life's joys and challenges, committed to one another.

VOW EXCHANGE

__________, please take you time and share your vows
__________, please share your vows.

Minister/Officiant:

__________, do you take __________, to live together in the union of marriage? To take him or her as your best friend and partner in life? To honor, cherish, and love him or her from this day forward, for better or for worse, for richer, for poor and sickness and in health for all your days? "I do"

__________, do you take __________, to live together in the union of marriage? to take care of her as your best friend and partner in life? To honor, cherish and love him or her from this day forward, for better, for worse, for richer, for poor, and sickness and in health for all of your days? "I do"

<h1 style="text-align:center">RING EXCHANGE</h1>

Please join hands.

Minister/Officiant:

The wedding rings circular shape represents the unending power of love and a source with no beginning and no end. You should wear these rings proudly and let them remind you each day of your commitment to one another.

__________, please take _________ left hand and when you are ready, please repeat after me.

I ________, give you _________, with this ring I wed you for today and all those that follow. As I place it on your finger, I give it as a symbol of my love and commitment to accept all that you are and have yet to be. Please wear as a notice to the entire world, that I am your husband.

__________, please take _________ left hand and when you are ready, please repeat after me.

I ________, give you _________, with this ring I wed you for today the tomorrow and all the years to come. As I place it on your finger, I give it as a symbol of my love and commitment to accept all that you are and have yet to be. Please wear as a notice to the entire world, that I am your wife.

<h1 style="text-align:center">CLOSING</h1>

Minister/Officiant:

Going forward knowing that you have chosen and been chosen. You no longer walk alone through life. To make your relationship work will take love. This is the core of your marriage and why you are here today. It will take trust, to know that in your hearts, you truly want what is best for each other.

Be each other's teachers and know that you are surrounded by people in this very space who love you. May you have many long years to delight in each other's love and company. I wish you the best through every season of your lives together.

By the power vested in me, by the state of Florida, I am overjoyed and honored to pronounce you are married, sealed together today both in law and in love.

__________ and ________, you may seal this marriage with a kiss.

Full Ceremony Script Sample

SAMPLE OF CEREMONY #2

Opening

Friends and family, we are gathered here today to celebrate the joining of Derek and K in marriage. Thank you for coming to witness their declaration of love for each other with this lifelong commitment.

The joining of two people in marriage is a historic tradition binding a couple together with their love and devotion to each other. The vows made today represent this commitment to their partner and serve as the foundation of their union.

Family Acknowledgment

Before we begin, let us take a moment to recognize the importance of family in this ceremony. Derek and K, please take a moment to turn and look at your guests. At this time, we would like to invite the family members of the couple to stand if you are able.

Family is an essential part of any marriage, especially for these two, and we recognize the role that your families have played in bringing you both to this point. They have nurtured you, supported you, and provided you with the foundation for the love and commitment that you share today. As we stand here today, surrounded by family and friends, they want to thank everyone for their love and support.

Friends and family, Derek and K have invited you here to witness this momentous occasion because they are so excited to start the next journey of their lives together. As they continue to support each other's dreams and passions, thank you for your presence as it is considered a blessing for their union. You may be seated.

Love Story

Derek and K's love story began in 2016 at MacDill Air Force Base, where they both worked. At first sight, Derek was immediately drawn to K's beautiful eyes and smile. As they got to know each other, he couldn't help but admire her determination and loyalty.

K, on the other hand, was taken by Derek's caring and protective nature. She appreciates his unwavering protection and knows she can always count on him. Through their love of bike riding and gardening, traveling, and enjoying Sunday brunch, these two quickly discovered love! One fine day during a walk near the romantic boardwalk of Lake Erie in Buffalo New York, Derek proposed and the rest is history!

Reading/Quote

As we reflect on the love these two people share for each other, I wish to share a quote from the ancient Chinese philosopher Lao Tzu:
"Being deeply loved by someone gives you strength while loving someone deeply gives you courage."
Despite this quote originating over two thousand years ago, this message still resonates today as the love between Derek and K gives them the strength and courage to face life's challenges head on, hand in hand, for years to come.

Address the Couple

By standing here together, you both are making promises to:

Create a good marriage by remembering the little things are the big things!
Be present in your union and showing up each day offering your love and support for your spouse.
Speak words of appreciation and demonstrate gratitude in thoughtful ways.
Grow together and provide a safe space for your love to endlessly blossom.

Vow Exchange, (if applicable)

Derek, please take your time and share your vows
K., please share your vows.

Derek and K, standing in the presence of your loved ones and in the embrace of this sacred union I invite you to look into each other 's eyes. Derek, do you, with all your heart, choose K as your partner in life, promising to honor, cherish, support, and provide love unconditionally? (I do)
K, do you, with all your heart, choose Derek as your partner in life, promising to honor, cherish, support, and provide love unconditionally? These responses will forever unite your spirits.

Ring Exchange

The wedding rings circular shape represents the unending power of love and a source with no beginning and no end. The rings you exchange today are the physical embodiment of the love you share. Whenever you look at your rings, remember the feelings you shared on this day and let the love and devotion you have right now, fill all the days of your marriage.

May we have the rings, please?
Derek, please take K. left hand and when you are ready, please repeat after me.

With this ring/I Derek/ wed you K./ for today and all those that follow/As I place it on your finger/ I give it as a symbol/ of my love and commitment/to accept all that you are/and have yet to become. Please wear as a notice/ to the entire world/that I am husband.

K., please take Derek left hand and when you are ready, please repeat after me.

With this ring/I K./ wed you Derek/ for today and all those that follow/As I place it on your finger/ I give it as a symbol/ of my love and commitment/to accept all that you are/and have yet to become. Please wear as a notice/ to the entire world/that I am your wife.

Closing

Going forward know that you have chosen each other. You no longer walk alone through life. To make your relationship work will take love. This is the core of your marriage and why you are here today. It will take trust to know that in your hearts, you truly want what is best for each other.

Derek and K. may your love continue to grow stronger with each day passing. May you continue to inspire each other, cultivate beautiful gardens, enjoy Sunday brunches and never stop traveling together. I ask that you always treat yourself and each other with respect and remind yourselves often of what brought you together today. Give the highest priority to the tenderness, gentleness, and kindness that your marriage deserves. Know you are stronger together than you are apart, and that for all your days you two will partake in all of life's joys and challenges, committed to one another.

By the power vested in me, by the state of Florida, I am overjoyed and honored to pronounce you are married, sealed together today both in law and in love. Derek, you may kiss your lovely bride.

Ladies and gentlemen, I present to you Mr. and Mrs. K.!

Processional Break Down

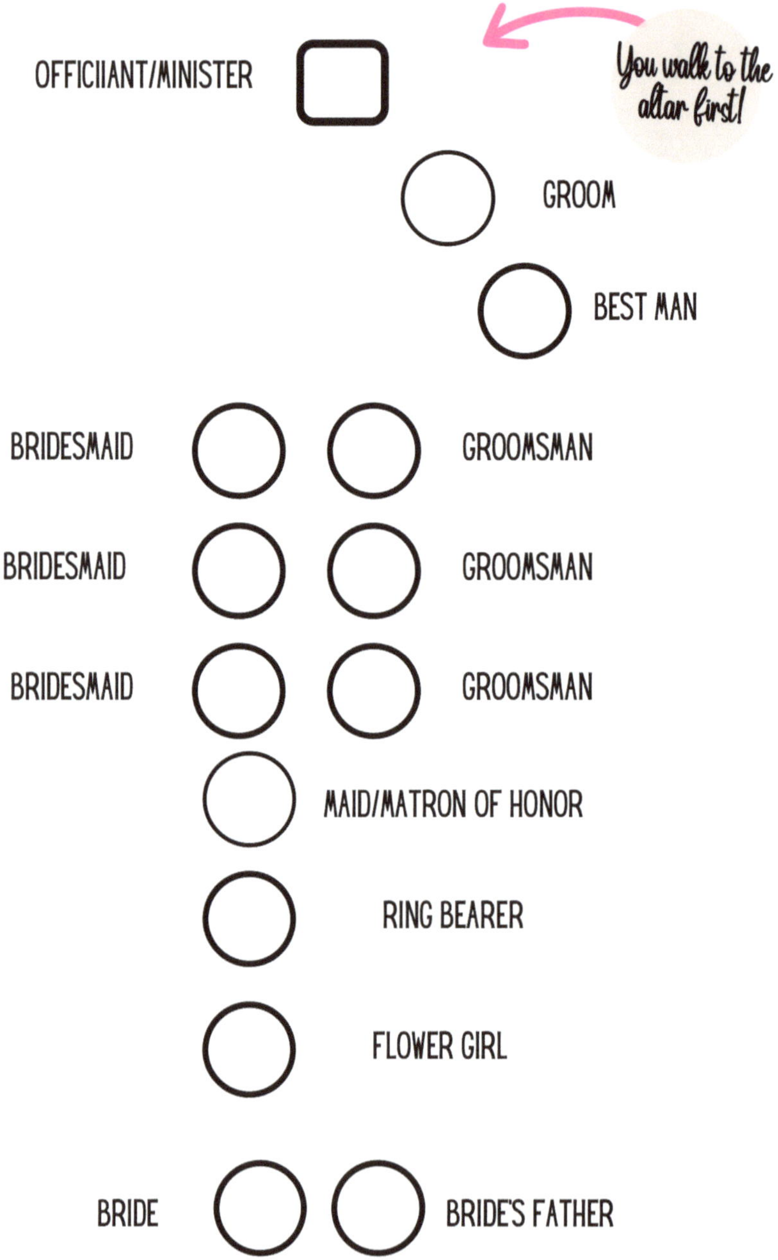

Recession Break Down

OFFICIIANT/MINISTER

BRIDESMAID — GROOMSMAN

BRIDESMAID — GROOMSMAN

BRIDESMAID — GROOMSMAN

RING BEARER

FLOWER GIRL

BRIDE — GROOM

Unique Options to Offer

Allow your couples to pick the day of their dreams with any of these!

- ☐ SAND CEREMONY
- ☐ HAND BLESSING
- ☐ CORD BRAIDING
- ☐ A SHOT OF LIQUOR
- ☐ PLANT A TREE
- ☐ WEDDING PRAYERS
- ☐ FEET WASHING
- ☐ RING WARMING
- ☐ CANDLE LIGHTING

- ☐ WINE & LOVE LETTER CAPSULE
- ☐ JUMPING THE BROOM
- ☐ CUP OF TEA OR COFFEE

Determine where to tie these into the ceremony

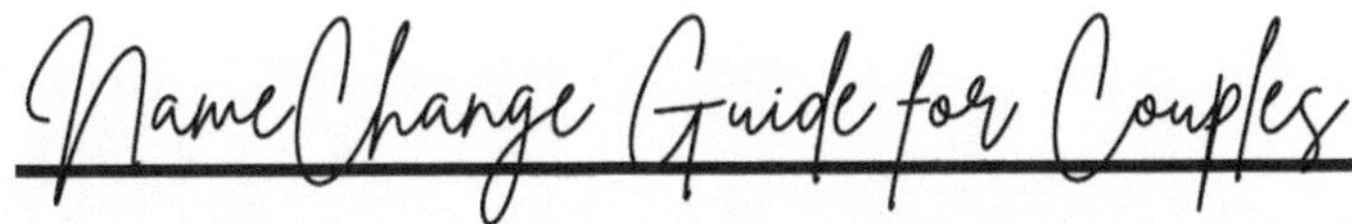

In **Florida**, couples who wish to change their last name after marriage can do so by following these steps:

1. Obtain a certified copy of the Marriage Certificate from the county clerk's office where the marriage license was issued.

2. Complete the "Petition for Change of Name" form, which can be found on the **Florida** courts website or obtained from the clerk's office. Both spouses will need to sign the form. (include this form with your complimentary certificate as a freebie)

3. File the completed form with the clerk of the circuit court in the county where they live. There will be a filing fee, which varies by county.

4. After filing the petition, the court will schedule a hearing, which both spouses must attend. At the hearing, the judge will ask questions to ensure that the name change is not being done for fraudulent purposes.

5. Once the judge approves the name change, the court will issue a court order. This order can be used to update name on legal documents, such as driver's license, social security card, and passport.

6. To update name on Driver's License, visit local Florida Department of Highway Safety and Motor Vehicles (DHSMV) office. Bring the court order, current driver's license, and proof of identity, such as a passport or birth certificate.

7. To update name on Social Security Card, complete an "Application for a Social Security Card" form and provide the court order, current social security card, and proof of identity, such as a passport or birth certificate. Then submit the application in person at a Social Security Administration office or by mail.

It's important to note that there are some restrictions on name changes in Florida. For example, you cannot change your name for fraudulent purposes, such as to evade debts or criminal prosecution. Additionally, you cannot change your name to one that includes any vulgar or obscene language.

Marriage Certificate Requests

A marriage certificate is a crucial document that legally proves the existence of a marriage. If you have recently tied the knot and need to request your marriage certificate, follow this step-by-step guide to make the process smooth and efficient:

1. Identify the Issuing Authority: This is typically the vital records office, county clerk's office, or registrar of marriages.

2. Gather Required Information: This may include the full names of both spouses, the date of marriage, the place of marriage, the name of the officiant, and any other details requested by the issuing authority.

3. Choose a Request Method: Common options include in-person applications, mail-in requests, online applications, or over-the-phone orders.

4. Fill Out the Application: If applying in person, the office staff may provide a physical application form to fill out. For online or mail-in requests, find a downloadable application on the issuing authority's website. Complete the application accurately and legibly.

5. Provide Supporting Documents: Check the specific requirements of issuing authority and include all necessary documents with your application.

6. Pay the Required Fees: Make sure to pay the specified amount by cash, check, credit card, or any other acceptable payment method. The fee can vary depending on location and whether you're requesting additional copies.

7. Submit the Application: Include all necessary documents and fees according to chosen method. In-person applications may be processed on the spot, while mail-in or online requests may take longer.

8. Processing Time: The time frame for processing marriage certificate requests can vary depending on location and the current workload of the issuing authority. In some cases, you may receive the certificate within a few days, while in others, it could take several weeks.

9. How the Certificate is Received: May vary based on chosen request method. For in-person requests, couples might be able to pick up the certificate directly from the office. For mail-in or online applications, the certificate will be mailed to the address provided in the application.

10. Secure and Use the Certificate: Upon receiving the marriage certificate, store it in a safe and secure location. Obtain multiple certified copies if needed for various legal purposes, such as changing names, updating identification, or applying for joint benefits.

Abundant Notary Services
Minister Courtney Baldwin
WINTER PARK, FL 32792
(407) 434-1660
courtneybaldwin@signaturebyans.com

This Agreement is made between Minister Courtney Baldwin and the Couple (as defined below), to retain an Officiant to perform a marriage license signing ceremony, elopement, or other marriage service as outlined below.

Courtney Baldwin is an inclusive & affirming officiant, and does not discriminate on the basis of race, color, religion(s), gender, national origin, disability, or sexual orientation. Your love is welcome here!

THE COUPLE

____
* Full Legal Name (as it appears on your ID & marriage license):

____
* Phone Number: ______________________
* Email address: ______________________
* Physical address:

____
____

____
* Full Legal Name (as it appears on your ID & marriage license):

____
* Phone Number: ______________________
* Email address: ______________________
* Physical address:

____
____

IMPORTANT: The Couple are responsible for obtaining their marriage license before the marriage ceremony. The Couple must bring their valid marriage license, valid photo ID for both parties, and 2 adult witnesses (optional) to the ceremony for the service to be legally binding.
Marrier #1 initial: __________________
Marrier #2 initial: __________________

THE WEDDING DETAILS
YOUR CEREMONY PACKAGE:
(See service terms below for details & requirements.)

Marriage License Signing ($150; no ceremony, 2 required witnesses)
Elopement Ceremony ($250; 30 minute ceremony & up to 1 one-hour consultation)
Vow Renewal Ceremony ($200; 30 minute ceremony & up to 2 one-hour consultations, no license signing)

Check this box if you'd need a list of vendors (photographers, bartenders, venues, etc) ☐

ADDITIONAL SERVICES:
Wedding Ceremony Script and/or Vow assistance ($150; as outlined below)
Rehearsal Ceremony ($75; One hour maximum, service recommended)
Wedding Add-ons ($75 per add-on unless included in selected ceremony package)
Travel fee (65.5 cents/mile added for all locations outside of Winter Park, FL)
Holiday fee ($75; for marriages performed on New Years Eve/Day, Labor Day, Memorial Day,
Halloween, Thanksgiving, or Christmas)

DATE, TIME, & LOCATION:
* Wedding date: ______
* Wedding venue (Name & Address)/Location:

____
____
* Your ceremony starts at: 0:00 (Circle: AM / PM)

Check this box if you'd need a list of vendors (photographers, bartenders, venues, etc)

IMPORTANT: If your ceremony starts more than 15 minutes late (after the time listed above), an
additional $50 will be charged for the Officiant's time. Ceremonies that start more than 30 minutes late
will only be performed if the Officiant's schedule permits.

SERVICE TERMS
CEREMONY PACKAGES & ADDITIONAL SERVICES:

* Marriage License Signing: Officiant will confirm the couple's identity and intent to marry and
complete the marriage license. This service is limited to 5-10 minutes and does not include a ceremony.
The Couple has the option to provide two adult witnesses and may invite up to four guests total
(including witnesses). The Officiant will return the license to the designated County Clerk's office
within 10 days of the ceremony, as required by Florida statute.

* Elopement or Traditional Ceremony: The Officiant agrees to arrive at the venue at least 30-60 minutes
before the ceremony start-time. The Officiant will perform a marriage ceremony for the Couple and
complete the marriage license. This service is limited to ceremonies up to 45 minutes long, not
including signing services. The Officiant will return the license to the County Clerk's office within 10
days of the ceremony, as required by Florida statute. In addition, the Officiant agrees to provide up to 2
hours of consultation time to plan the ceremony and review the wedding script (either over video,
phone, or in-person).

* Vow Renewal Ceremony: The Officiant agrees to arrive at the venue at least 30-60 minutes before the
ceremony start-time. The Officiant agrees to perform a vow renewal ceremony for the Couple. This
service does not include a marriage license signing service. This service is limited to ceremonies up to
45 minutes long. In addition, the Officiant agrees to provide up to 2 hours of consultation time to plan
the ceremony and review the wedding script (either over video, phone, or in-person).

* Custom Wedding Ceremony Script and/or Vows: Officiant agrees to write a custom wedding ceremony
script and/or wedding vows for the Couple, provided that the Couple completes and returns the
Couple's Questionnaire at least 2 weeks before the wedding date. The Couple can request up to 2 script
revisions, after which time an additional fee of $100 will be charged per revision. No revision requests
will be accepted within 3 days of the ceremony.

* Rehearsal Ceremony: The Officiant agrees to attend a rehearsal ceremony for up to one hour, dressed in casual attire. This service does not include organizing or leading a rehearsal ceremony; the Officiant will attend in a limited capacity to review the wedding ceremony order and any unity ceremony components. Additional travel fees may apply (at 65.5 cents/ mile; per the IRS 2023 standard mileage rate).

COST OF SERVICES
DEPOSIT REQUIREMENT & PAYMENT SCHEDULE

Cost Breakdown:
Service Package: $_____
Additional Services (combined): $ 0.00
Estimated Convenience Fee: $_______
Total Cost for Services: $______

Deposit Requirement:
The Couple agrees to pay a deposit in the amount of $100 upon signing this agreement. This deposit will be put toward the total owed and places a 'hold' on the Officiant's services on the wedding date given herein. This deposit is non-refundable, with few exceptions (see Cancellation policies for more information).

Remaining Balance:
The Couple agrees to pay the remaining balance for all services before _________ (72 business hours before your wedding date).

Payments must be made via Zelle to: <u>abundantnotaryservices@gmail.com</u>, unless otherwise stated or discussed.

IMPORTANT: The Couple is responsible for providing any special materials they wish to use in the marriage ceremony, such as unity candles, unity sand, handfasting cords, wedding rings, etc.

CANCELLATION & CHANGE POLICY
IF THE COUPLE CANCELS OR REQUESTS A DATE/TIME/LOCATION CHANGE:
A Couple is not required to pay the remaining balance on services if they cancel at least 1 week before the scheduled ceremony. If the balance has already been paid, it will be returned if the cancellation occurs at least 1 week before the scheduled ceremony. Changes to a Couple's wedding date, ceremony start time, or location (outside Winter Park) will only be accommodated as the Officiant's availability allows. If the ceremony cannot be satisfactorily rescheduled, cancellation guidelines will apply. Deposits are non-refundable except in extreme circumstances, such as severe weather (see below) or when either party to the marriage must be hospitalized for severe illness/injury before the ceremony can occur.

IF THE OFFICIANT CANCELS:
If the Officiant is unable to perform a Couple's ceremony due to illness, family emergency, or other unforeseen circumstance, an authorized Backup Officiant will be provided in their place. The Backup Officiant will be given full access to all ceremony planning materials, custom ceremony script (if applicable), etc, and will perform the Officiant's duties as defined above in full. If the Couple chooses to hire an alternate replacement officiant on their own, the Couple will be given full access to any custom ceremony materials to use. If the Officiant delays the start of the wedding (due to late arrival, etc.) the Couple will be refunded 25% of the total ceremony cost.

IF MOTHER NATURE CANCELS:
Ceremonies that must be canceled or rescheduled due to extreme weather or unsafe conditions affecting the venue and surrounding areas, such as tornadoes, hurricanes, flooding, fire, or severe heat/cold, are fully refundable (excluding the deposit) and can be rescheduled with the Officiant based on availability.

SIGNATURES
Please sign and date below.

By signing this contract, I have read and understand the terms and conditions outlined above.

THE OFFICIANT
Printed Name: Courtney Baldwin
Signature: ____
Date: ______________

____
Printed Name: _______________________________________
Signature: ____
Date: ______________

____
Printed Name: _______________________________________
Signature: ____
Date: ______________

[Your Name or Company Name]
[Address]
[City, State, ZIP]
[Email Address]
[Phone Number]
[Website]

PHOTO RELEASE FORM

I, [Couple's Name], hereby grant permission to [Your Name or Company Name], to use photographs of us taken on the day of the ceremony, reception, rehearsals, or other related events, for the purpose of promotional materials, advertising, and social media content.

Terms and Conditions:
1. The couple's wishes and preferences regarding the use of their photographs, decorations, or any other related images will be respected by [Your Name or Company Name] to the best of our ability.

2. [Your Name or Company Name] will use the photographs solely for marketing and promotional purposes, such as on our website, social media platforms, brochures, business cards, advertising campaigns, or any other relevant marketing material we may create.

3. Unlimited usage rights are granted to [Your Name or Company Name], including, but not limited to, reproducing, distributing, displaying, and publishing the photographs on various platforms.

4. The couple retains the right to request the removal of their photographs from any platform or marketing material at any time. Upon receiving such a request, [Your Name or Company Name] will promptly remove the images from our platforms, and cease further usage in future marketing campaigns.

5. The couple acknowledges that once images are posted on public social media platforms, they may be shared or reproduced by third parties over whom [Your Name or Company Name] has no control. Therefore, [Your Name or Company Name] cannot be held responsible for any unauthorized use or reproduction of the photographs by third parties.

6. The couple voluntarily provides a release for [Your Name or Company Name] of any liability for claims by the couple or any third party in relation to the use of the photographs as described in this form.

By signing below, I, [Couple's Name], confirm that I have read and understood the terms stated in this photo release form, and I grant permission for [Your Name or Company Name] to use the photographs in accordance with the conditions outlined above.

Date: [Date]

Couple's Name: _______________________________________
(Couple's Signature)

Wedding Officiant/Company Representative: _______________
(Officiant/Representative's Signature)

ABOUT THE AUTHOR

Courtney Baldwin is a multi-talented entrepreneur, life coach and author who has made a name for herself in a variety of fields. Since her passion is helping others she began her career in the financial aid industry and working tirelessly to help students achieve their dreams of higher education.

She became an autodidact, voraciously consuming books and online resources on a variety of subjects. This newfound passion eventually led her to become a wedding officiant, where she finds great joy in helping couples celebrate their love and commitment.

Today, Baldwin is a successful entrepreneur, author, life coach, and wedding officiant. She has helped countless clients overcome obstacles and unlock their full potential, and her work still continues.

Baldwin is also a sought-after speaker and thought leader, regularly appearing at seminars and events to share her insights and inspire others to pursue their passions.

You can follow her on Instagram @abundantnotaryservicesbyco